"THE REDEEMER -
THE REDEEMED"

BY

HENRY D. HOUGHTON

THE COVENANT PUBLISHING CO. LTD.
121, Low Etherley, Bishop Auckland, Co. Durham, DL14 0HA
2011

Third Edition 2011

ISBN 978-085205-089-7

Printed by
THE COVENANT PUBLISHING COMPANY LIMITED
121, Low Etherley, Bishop Auckland,
Co. Durham, DL14 0HA
www.covpub.co.uk

THE REDEEMER – THE REDEEMED

CHAPTER I

Of all the glorious names applied in the Scriptures to our Lord Jesus Christ, none stands out with such brilliance and such loveliness as this-"THE REDEEMER!"

It is a wonderful word, describing most fully His work as well as Him.

It is heard in our prayers, it is heard in our songs, it is heard in our exhortations.

It is the light upon the hill, it is the Star in the night, it is the Sun at noon! It is the glory that excelleth!

And yet it is greatly to be questioned whether we have rightly understood it.

It seems like the name that is above every name, yet it is not. For it is not the same *"Redeemer"* at which *every knee is to bow*. It is at the name of *"Jesus."* Both to the Gentiles and Israel that is His saving name. But to Israel He is also "THY REDEEMER." What does it mean?

It seems very unorthodox to say that the Gentiles are not and cannot be redeemed. Yet it is perfectly true.

To them Christ is offered as their Saviour, and all may accept Him who will, but to Israel there is to come through that same Christ a national redemption.

"But when the fullness of the time was come, God sent forth His Son, made under law" (what for? To redeem the Gentiles? Oh, no)

"to redeem them that were under the law."

This shows the redemption coming to those **under the law**. These could not be Gentiles! The law had nothing to say to them. And St. Paul says that was the purpose of Christ's coming.

This agrees most particularly with Christ's own announcement, *"I am not sent but unto the lost sheep of the house of Israel."* And that other strange command of our Lord viewed in the light of the theology of today, "Go not into the way of the Gentiles, and into any city of the Samaritans enter ye not: *but go rather to the lost sheep of the house of Israel" Matthew* 10:5-6.

And most assuredly He did not mean the Jews, as St. John plainly indicates.

"But though He had done so many miracles before them, yet they believed not on Him: That the saying of Esaias the prophet might be fulfilled, which he spake, Lord, who hath believed our report? . . . *Therefore they could not believe, because that Esaias said again, He hath blinded their eyes, and hardened their heart; that they should not see with their eyes, nor understand with their heart, and be converted, and I should heal them" John* 12:37-40.

And *Matthew* 13:10-11, corroborates. "And the disciples came, and unto Him, Why speakest thou unto them in parables? He answered and said unto them, *Because it is given unto you to know the mysteries of the kingdom of heaven, but unto them it is not given."* Therefore, and indisputably, these could not be the people to whom He was sent.

We use the term, *"The* Redeemer," indicating the one and only Redeemer. But God says in speaking to Israel, "THY REDEEMER."

"For thy Maker is thine husband; the LORD of hosts is his name, and THY REDEEMER, the Holy One of Israel . . . For the Lord hath called thee as a woman forsaken . . . For a small moment have I forsaken thee; but with great mercies will I gather thee. In a little wrath I hid my face from thee for a moment; but with everlasting kindness will I have mercy on thee, saith the LORD THY REDEEMER" *Isaiah* 54:5-8.

All this is spoken to *the desolate, the widow* full of shame and reproach as vv. 1 to 4 tells us, and could not possibly fit the latter day Christian Church. God has never hidden His face from the true Church, nor been wrath with it, nor treated it as a shameless forsaken woman. But He did Israel, for she deserved it!

But all this is a work of redemption performed for Israel nationally, a renewing, a restoration, which is not thoroughly entered into or even perceived yet.

In *Isaiah* 49:25-26, we have a very forceful and pronounced statement, referring to those who had been carried away captive. "But thus saith the LORD, Even the captives of the mighty shall be taken away, and the prey of the terrible shall be delivered: for I will contend with him that contendeth with thee, and I will save thy children . . . *And all flesh shall know*" (then this thing is not going to be done in a corner, **all flesh shall know**) "*that I the LORD am thy Saviour and thy Redeemer, the mighty One of Jacob.*"

Again these words "Thy Redeemer."

We have in *Isaiah* 44:21-22 words addressed to Israel by name, showing their redemption, even though they had not turned unto God. "Remember these, O Jacob and Israel; for thou art My servant . . . O Israel, thou shalt not be forgotten of me. I have blotted out, as thick as a cloud, thy transgressions, and, as a cloud, thy sins: *return unto me*," (this shows she is still estranged from God, so cannot be the Church, and yet there follows these words) "*for I have redeemed thee.*"

This is not an isolated quotation by any means. Take *Isaiah* 48:20. "Declare ye, tell this, utter it even to the end of the earth; say ye, *The LORD hath redeemed His servant Jacob.*" This is something so delightful to God, that proclamation is to be made of it to the ends of the earth. Again, "Fear thou not, thou worm Jacob, and ye men of Israel;" (is that clear?) "I will help thee, saith the LORD, *and thy Redeemer, the Holy One of Israel" Isaiah* 41:14.

But wise men today say, "That God will not redeem Israel," they say those old promises are now impossible of fulfilment.

What does the Psalmist say? "Let Israel hope in the LORD: for with the LORD there is mercy, and with Him is plenteous redemption. *And He shall redeem Israel from all his iniquities" Psalm* 130:7-8.

Perhaps someone says, "That is the Old Testament, can you show us Israel's redemption from the New?" Yes indeed! Zacharias, the father of John the Baptist, "Filled with the Holy Ghost, and prophesied, saying, *Blessed be the Lord God of Israel; for He hath visited and redeemed* HIS PEOPLE, . . . *as he spake by the mouth of his holy prophets, which have been since the world began . . . to perform the mercy promised to our fathers, and to remember His holy covenant" Luke* 1:67-72.

Surely that is clear. "Redeemed His People!"

And please give due credence to our Lord's words:

"I am not sent but unto the lost sheep of the house of Israel" *Matthew* 15:24.

And surely, surely, our Lord knew why He was sent and to whom He was sent.

But St. Paul has something to say, "Christ hath **redeemed** us from the curse of the law (the condemnation of the law), being made a curse for us" *Galatians* 3:13.

Note, only those under the law could be redeemed from it.

And again in *Romans* 11:26.

"And so all Israel shall be saved: as it is written, *There shall come out of Sion the Deliverer, and shall turn away ungodliness from Jacob.*"

This is a quotation from *Isaiah* 59:20: "And the Redeemer shall come to Zion, and unto them that turn from transgression in Jacob, saith the LORD." And St. Paul declares its truth, and quotes it as being certain of fulfilment, and he finishes, "for this is my covenant unto them, when I shall take away their sins."

This could not mean the Jews, for when the Redeemer came they seized Him and slew Him. They could not be those who turn from transgression in Jacob: and alas that attitude continues to this day. It is some other section of the nation of which it is speaking.

We may learn something of what that word "Redeem" means by referring to *Exodus* 13:13. The word is used here in a very strange connection.

"*And every firstling of an ass thou shalt redeem with a lamb; and if thou wilt not redeem it, then thou shalt break his neck.*"

Here man had to do the redeeming by offering another's life.

By the compassionate reckoning of God an inferior life was accepted instead of the superior, and was to redeem that superior.

It was so with Abraham and Isaac. "And Abraham lifted up his eyes, and looked, and behold behind him a ram caught in a thicket by his horns: and Abraham went and took the ram, *and offered him up for a burnt-offering in the stead of his son*" *Genesis* 22:13.

That was the first redeeming, as in Jesus was the last.

Failing the redeeming lamb, the ass was to be killed. So then it meant in that case to save from physical death.

Only by the compassionate reckoning and appointment of God could the inferior be accepted as a ransom for the superior.

But when the final redemption was accomplished, it was quite the contrary. *The Superior died for the inferior*!

The Greater for the less, the Sinless for the sinful.

Here is no favouritism in the reckoning! *The full price is paid-* **and more**! The Just for the unjust!

Now there is nothing in our national life to show us the full meaning of redemption as there was to the Hebrews.

The eldest born male of man was commanded to be redeemed: for the very same verse which commands the offering of the lamb to redeem the firstling of the ass, goes on to say, *"And all the firstborn of man among thy children shalt thou redeem."* And this redeeming was at the cost of a life!

While there are cases in Scripture of lesser meaning, yet the chief teaching of the Book is that to redeem is to give a life for another's.

Even our Lord when He was born was taken to the Temple with the offering, a pair of turtledoves or two young pigeons, *the redemption price according to the Law of Moses*. For every first-born male among men had to be redeemed, and God tells us why in *Exodus* 13. That they may keep in everlasting remembrance the saving of Israel's firstborn when those of the Egyptians were slain at the first Passover.

Two of the disciples on the way to Emmaus said to our risen Lord, *"We trusted that it had been He which should have redeemed Israel."* **And it was!**

But they could not see that redeeming was by death: though there had been 1500 years of sacrifices to teach them. *To redeem is to die for*! They knew that by their sacrifices but failed to apply it, even as some fail to apply it today.

But it says, *"To redeem Israel."* Now this cannot mean "Those who will become an "Israel" by being redeemed."

It is some work performed for the nation as a whole. And I would suggest that it is effective and active to full accomplishment for them whether they know it or not.

The announcements of it in the Old Testament *are all surprise announcements*!

Listen to this: "Thus saith the LORD, Ye have sold yourselves for nought; *and ye shall be redeemed without money"* Isaiah 52:3.

And again, "O Israel, Fear not: for *I have redeemed thee"* Isaiah 43:1.

And again, "I will hiss for them and gather them, *for I have redeemed them."*

Again note the overwhelming surprise of this announcement, *"And your covenant with death shall be disannulled, and your agreement with hell shall not stand"* Isaiah 28:18. There is the Redeeming though the word is not used.

Again, "I will ransom them from the power of the grave; I will redeem them from death" *Hosea* 13:14. And undoubtedly this is Israel, see verse 9.

CHAPTER II

Just before our Lord Jesus Christ was crucified, while the chief Priests and the Pharisees were holding their Council, there occurred an incident which is most enlightening.

Caiaphas was the High Priest, the highest authority in the nation: he was not a prophet, and yet he was chosen to give to the nation a most remarkable prophecy.

Addressing the assembled Council he said: "Ye know nothing at all, nor consider that it is expedient for us, that one man should die for the people, and that the whole nation perish not."

But the inspired record goes on: - "*And this spake he not of himself: but being high priest that year, he prophesied that Jesus should die for that nation.*"

You have their substitution, you have their atonement, you have their redemption!

Mark the significance of the fact that the High Priest, the highest ecclesiastical authority, was chosen by God to make this strange declaration. Our Lord was living, but He did not make the announcement! All the disciples were living, but they were not chosen! Why the High Priest? It was an announcement by the properly constituted authority of the one offering, for the sins of the people!

Nor was it to be confined to that small portion of the nation then in Palestine, for the Word expressly makes the declaration wide enough to include all those, their brothers, long before scattered among the nations. For it says: - "*And not for that nation only, but that also He should gather together in one the children of God that were scattered abroad.*"

Now it is evident that this was a message to the nation, the twelve-tribed nation, and it was given to the High Priest as the representative of that nation that he might deliver it.

But look at it. "One man die for the people."

"The whole nation perish not." The whole principle of redemption is there! And he applied it to that nation - wicked, disobedient, Christ-hating as it was, and St. John applies it also to the brother people, *"The children of God,"* who were at that time scattered abroad.

But who were these *"Children of God"*? Certainly not the Gentiles: *for to them as yet salvation had not been offered*! But call to mind those tremendous words of Moses, spoken to the old Israel nation, *"Ye are the children of the LORD your God" Deuteronomy* 14:1. There is the explanation!

There we have *"The children of God"* who were scattered abroad!

Remember that the Jews had previously said of Christ, "Will He go unto the dispersed among the Gentiles?" *John* 7:35.

The R. V., Ferrar Fenton, and Weymouth all say "The Dispersion," evidently referring to the scattering of the old house of Israel. And St. Peter addresses his first epistle to this same people.

But the High Priest said that *"He should gather together in one the children,"* etc. One what? One nation surely! And if so, this corresponds exactly with *Ezekiel* 37:22-24, "And I will make them" (Israel and Judah) *"one nation* in the land upon the mountains of Israel; and one king shall be king to them all: and they shall be no more two nations, neither shall they be divided into two kingdoms any more at all . . . And David my servant shall be king over them." In all this we can see the House of Israel coming back into the line of blessing through Jesus Christ, exactly as had been promised.

There is, however, another very singular and beautiful passage which confirms all this.

"And now, saith the LORD that formed me from the womb to be his servant, *to bring Jacob again to Him*" (notice that word "*again*" showing that it is the same Jacob who had gone astray), "Though Israel be not gathered, yet shall I be glorious in the eyes of the LORD . . . And he said, It is (or margin "Art thou") a light thing that thou shouldest be my servant to *raise up the tribes of Jacob, and to restore the preserved of Israel*: I will also give thee for a light to the Gentiles, that thou mayest be my salvation unto the end of the earth" *Isaiah* 49:5-6.

The writer would humbly suggest that "The Servant" is the Lord Jesus Christ, who is "To bring Jacob again to Him" (God) "and to raise up the tribes of Jacob, and to restore the preserved of Israel," as well as to be a Light to the Gentiles.

Or to give Ferrar Fenton's version: -
"I made you my agent to raise Jacob's standard, to lead Israel back, be a light to the heathen, and a Saviour to be to the bounds of the earth."

All this is in exact confirmation of the redeeming of Israel, and the bringing of Israel under the New Covenant. And further *it proves that Christ is the means whereby Ten-Tribed Israel is brought back again to God*, restored to His favour, and also to her original place and position, as well as to become a Saviour to the Gentiles.

It is also in exact agreement with our Saviour's declaration as to the purpose of His coming: and also that other misunderstood passage, "A light to lighten the Gentiles and the glory of Thy people Israel." Indeed it is no doubt a prediction of all this.

Seeing that this is so, it proves that lost Israel is to be, before she is brought back, the leading Christian nation of the world, and there is only one such.

Now let us look at something else.

A few years ago a gentleman at Swanwick startled me by this tremendous question:

"Why was it necessary that Judas should betray our Lord?"

To that I immediately replied: "It was not necessary."

It was no necessary part of the Eternal purpose of God that the traitor Judas should betray our Lord.

It was no necessary part of the Eternal purpose that the Jews should pile up their sin by crucifying Him!

Do you think it was God who prompted the rabble to cry out "Crucify Him! Crucify Him?" *It was not, it was The Devil!*

God's purposes could have been accomplished and would have been accomplished, without sin, if the Jews had not been so violent in their terrible and bitter hatred of our Lord.

The iniquity of the Jews was being filled up.

The vileness of man was being displayed in the most terrible form that this earth has ever known!

Was it necessary? No! No!

Listen to St. Peter's charge against the Jews.

"The God of our fathers hath glorified His Son Jesus, whom ye have delivered up, and denied Him in the presence of Pilate, when he was determined to let Him go.
But ye denied the Holy One and the Just, and desired a murderer to be granted unto you, and **killed the prince of life.**"

What a fearful charge!

St. Peter does not there charge Pilate with the murder of Jesus, *but the Jews*, and in the same passage he calls Jesus, *"God's Son,"* and also names Him, "The *Prince of Life."*

Was this villainy necessary? No! No! It was superfluous! It was man's cup of guilt being filled to the brim, and running over, unnecessarily so, for God could have accomplished all His purposes without the aid of sin!

Right from childhood there has seemed to the writer much unnecessary suffering about the crucifixion of our Lord.

If the victim, the Substitute, had to die, so let it be, but why the cruelty, the badgering, the smiting, the shame and spitting, the plucking-off of the hair, why the cruel crowns of thorns, *why the cross at all?*

Surely, surely, these superfluous indignities were no part of the necessary expiation.

The types and shadows did not foreshow anything of these, though the prophecies did.

The types showed what ought to come, and what was necessary, but that awful day exhibited a diabolical hatred, an intense fury utterly unnecessary, and altogether opposed to the spirit of sacrifice.

Why the Cross, the nails, the public exhibition as a common felon between two thieves? *This had no atoning value, this could not wipe out a single sin.*

The writer to the Hebrews says, "Without shedding of blood is no remission." But even he puts no value or merit upon the cruelty!

All the long line of sacrifices from Abraham's ram downwards had foreshown that the substitute must die, *but not cruelty, not disgrace, not horrid torture*! That was utterly and altogether contrary to the whole spirit of sacrifice and expiation!

What would have been thought of the heartless Priest who wilfully and persistently tortured the sacrificial offering?

Many years ago it was the writer's privilege to meet a very remarkable man in South Wales, and in his own house he gave him the following theory of the atonement. Only a theory, yet it might be true, at any rate it was so striking as to have stuck to the writer all these years, and certainly magnifies God as well as adds additional condemnation to man. Here it is, as near as may be.

"The old sacrifices and offerings of the children of Israel are plainly spoken of in all the Scriptures as pointing to and foreshadowing the great Sacrifice that was to come.

"So then, the types being in existence, and appointed by God, mark that it is fair to suppose that the Antitype when it came would follow along the prepared and prefigured lines.

"The Passover lamb (a male of the first year) was to be set apart quietly and deliberately according to the commandment. Then, when the proper and correct time had come it was taken, not in passion, nor in excitement of enmity or hatred, and its life taken mercifully and quickly in the appointed way.

"Now as all these types and symbols pointed on to the great Sacrifice, it is fair to assume that if the sacrifice prefigured had been allowed to proceed to its appointed end it would have been something like this:

"One certain day would have been appointed, perhaps months beforehand, for the great Passover Sacrifice in the which the one offering for sins for ever should be accomplished.

"All the nation, men, women, children, would be commanded to be present, and in some vast natural amphitheatre witness the offering of the one great Substitute for the sins of Israel, and for all mankind.

"There they stand, the High Priest and the Victim in the centre, the chiefs of the people all round Him, and round them the whole nation, as commanded, looking on.

"No noise, except the sound of weeping, no clamouring for the blood of the Victim, *but a fearful and overwhelming sorrow upon them all that their sins necessitated such a sacrifice.*

"Then, in sight of them all, the High Priest reluctantly yet obediently and mercifully takes the life of the One Offering: *and thus would their sins have been atoned for exactly according to plan and type.*

"In some such way would the great Offering have been made if it had run along the prefigured course, the High Priest as God's official representative, and also the representative of the nation, performing the rite according to the law!

"But, alas, the Jews did not allow it to proceed to this end.

"Enraged and full of malice they seized Him and caused Him violently and without reason to be put to death.

"The Lamb provided was not allowed to be quietly and peacefully offered, but by cruel hands was crucified and slain.

"*The Substitute, the Redeemer, the Lamb was seized in anger and in passion and was deliberately and of set purpose murdered, the High Priest aiding and abetting!*

"The Lamb long foretold as a Sacrifice for sin was taken and crucified as a common felon! Tragedy upon tragedy!

"Listen to that awful cry, *"His blood be upon us and upon our children."*

"Well might the Saviour say, "They know not what they do," and they did not."

In some such way did my friend suggest that the types should and probably would have been fulfilled, except for the wickedness and the malice of men, anticipating and preventing a calm and ordered offering of the Great Sacrifice for sin.

CHAPTER III

B ut what is the redeeming of Israel? Most assuredly it is something above and beyond anything taught in our churches.

It is not the bringing back of Israel to God's favour for her to be a wicked, sinful, rebellious people as of yore.

It is eventually and finally **the conversion of the whole nation!** Please set that sown. There are no clearer statements in the whole of God's Word than these. So then there is a time coming when the whole nation, men, women, children are to be brought to know God, actually, really and experimentally.

"This shall be the covenant that I will make with the house of Israel; After those days, saith the LORD, *I will put my law in their inward parts, and write it in their hearts*" (this is not man reforming, but a work done by God alone) . . . "And they shall teach no more every man his neighbour, and every man his brother, saying, Know the LORD, *for they shall all know me, from the least of them unto the greatest of them, saith the LORD*" *Jeremiah* 31:33-34. And in the whole of this great company there is not a single exception mentioned.

All this is spoken of *"The house of Israel."* Some, however, think that Judah is included because of what is said in verse 31.

He would, however, be a bold man that suggested that these words were spoken or predicted of pure Gentiles. God does, however, take out of the Gentiles a people for His name, but this passage does not refer to them. It says, *"The house of Israel."*

Again, God says through *Ezekiel* 39:7, "so will I make my holy name known *in the midst of my people Israel; and I will not let them pollute my holy name any more.*"

Again, God speaking through *Jeremiah* 32:39-40 says, "And I will give them one heart, and one way, that they may fear me for ever, for the good of them, and of their children after them . . . But *I will put my fear in their hearts, that they shall not depart from me.*" Here is God at work!

Again in *Ezekiel*: "Then *will* I sprinkle clean water upon you, and ye shall be clean: from all your filthiness, and from all your idols, *will* I cleanse you. A new heart also *will* I give you, and a new spirit *will* I put within you: and I *will* take away the stony heart out of your flesh, and I *will* give you an heart of flesh. And I *will* put my spirit within you, *and cause you to walk in my statutes, and ye shall keep my judgments, and do them.*"

And this cannot mean the Christian Church, for it goes on, "And ye shall dwell in the land that I gave to your fathers" *Ezekiel* 36:25-28.

Nor is this an experience which only one in ten thousand may enter into, but it is the settled ordinary condition *of everyone in the nation*!

Faith is not mentioned as a condition, love is not, and even hope is not!

There is no condition of any kind either stated or implied. It is a work to be accomplished by God just as much as when He made the world. And it is as sure and as certain as the world He made.

Further, it is not because all the bad are destroyed, and only the one in ten thousand left. That would be a strange redeeming of Israel.

Oh, no! Make no mistake; God is going to make His saints out of His sinners! And the achievement will be so notable that God will get to Himself greater renown by it than by anything the world has ever known.

In this short quotation God seven times declares that this work is His own: "WILL I," "I WILL." This is the "I will" of God and no man may break or hinder it.

If only those of extraordinary faith entered in, few would partake! But *all* partake, ALL are sharers, and it comes at a certain pre-arranged time: "**Then**," or as some passages say, "*In that day.*"

Now turn to *Hosea* 2:19-20, "*And I will betroth thee unto me for ever:*" (this is Israel, the Ten-Tribed house as proved by vv. 1, 2.) "*Yea, I will betroth thee unto me in righteousness, and in judgment, and in loving kindness, and in mercies. I will even betroth thee unto me in faithfulness: and thou shalt know the LORD.*"

Again, the "*I wills*" of God, showing what He is going to do, whether man pleases or not, and even despite our misunderstanding and our unbelief.

CHAPTER IV

Now let us consider the greatness of our inheritance,

There is more in British-Israel Truth than even the British-Israel Leaders have yet seen. We have seen *the fact, but the consequences are mightier, more profound, more far-reaching than the clearest-sighted man has yet perceived.*

We are like the long-lost son, who just found, and, coming home, is too delighted to be at home to think and wonder what the family estate is like.

But they take him to the palace windows to show it to him, and he says in admiration when he sees it, *"What a glorious estate!"*

But the servants say, "Wait a bit, you have not seen it yet. It goes beyond that hill, and the next hill, and the next:" and then he sits down and wonders. We are just like that son. We can see a little bit of the estate, and the bit we can see makes us sit down and wonder. We can see passages in the deeds in the Covenants which have a meaning far beyond anything we had imagined. *And we wonder whether it means all it says.* We can see it is big, something bigger than our previous conception, *but how big, how far out of sight it goes, we cannot, dare not, say!*

What about the great estate shown to us in *Ezekiel* 37? and *Jeremiah* 31? Can we see beyond the first hill, and the next, to the ultimate hill? What about those stirring words in *Isaiah* 62:2-3? "And the Gentiles shall see *thy righteousness,* and all kings *thy glory*: and thou shalt be called by a new name, which the mouth of the LORD shall name. *Thou shalt also be a crown of glory in the hand of the LORD, and a royal diadem in the hand of thy God."* Is there any second hill and third hill there as yet completely hidden from our feeble sight?

And those other words in verse 12 of the same chapter: "And they shall call them, *The holy people, the redeemed of the LORD,"* and verse 5: "As the bridegroom rejoiceth over the bride, so shall thy God rejoice over thee." Is there any ultimate hill there as yet not seen? And coming down to the New Testament, have we seen all there is in those strange words of St. Paul in *Romans* 11:26?

"And so all Israel shall be saved: as it is written, There shall come out of Sion the Deliverer, *and shall turn away ungodliness from Jacob . . ."*

Is there any second hill there? Is there any third hill there which we have not seen?

And that very beautiful chapter *Isaiah* 35, so much read, so little understood, beginning; "The wilderness and the solitary place shall be glad *for them*; and the desert shall rejoice, and blossom as the rose." And ending: "And the ransomed of the LORD shall return, and come to Zion with songs and everlasting joy upon their heads: they shall obtain joy and gladness, and sorrow and sighing shall flee away."

Is there any second and third hill there which we have not seen?

And so we might go on the whole book through! The inheritance is big beyond our utmost thought, we can see that it is, but *how much* bigger we do not know!

Some of our British-Israel writers have been anxious lest we should claim too much as the outcome of Israel's redemption. On the contrary we have not claimed enough! Or to put it a better way: our *claims have been and are infinitely below the clear statements of God's word*!

Some have suggested that the redemption of Israel was simply a bringing back to the land. Is that it which excites the unbounded and tumultuous joy of God at its contemplation as described in His word? Surely not! *God could have brought them back at any time.*

But that was not His only purpose. God had His great work to do not only *for* Israel, but *in* Israel.

Listen to these great words of God, and say whether you do not see there something more than a return from captivity:

"But Israel shall be *saved in the LORD with an everlasting salvation*: ye shall not be ashamed nor confounded world without end" *Isaiah* 45:17. That is much more than a mere earthly deliverance. It speaks of being "s*aved in the Lord,*" and "*With an everlasting salvation.*" Almost the identical words we should use today to describe a person's change of heart and life! And further it lasts forever, "*World without end.*"

We have there not only the heart conversion of Israel, *but of every man, woman and child therein.*

And, if it is doubted, look at the last verse in the same chapter. "*In the LORD shall all the seed of Israel be justified, and shall glory.*"

"*Be justified?*" The very thing which St. Paul afterwards preached, "Justification by faith." But here it says that "*all the seed of Israel shall be justified.*" What can you make of that? This justification is the bringing back of the mind and soul and purpose of the whole of Israel to God. And the closing words confirm it all, "*And shall glory.*"

This is Israel glorying, and rejoicing in God. And in the previous chapter we have God glorying in Israel.

"Thou art My servant: O Israel, thou shalt not be forgotten of me. I have blotted out, as a thick cloud, thy transgressions, and, as a cloud, thy sins: return unto me; *for I have redeemed thee*" Isaiah 44:21-22.

The Redeeming is connected with the blotting out of the sins! *The Redeeming brings the blotting out!* And it speaks of it as so certain in the future that it says "*I have blotted out.*" What can you do with that?

If God says, "*I have blotted out,*" and "*I have redeemed thee,*" there is no more to be said. And the passage finishes with God glorying in the Israel He has redeemed.

"For the LORD hath redeemed Jacob, and glorified himself in Israel," v. 23.

If God has blotted out Israel's sins, if He has redeemed Israel, surely that points to Israel's salvation *yet to be accomplished.*

We have seen these things in the Bible many times, but we have not understood them, or rather have not believed them.

But they are there, and are part and parcel of the Word of Truth which our Lord endorsed when He said "*Thy word is Truth:*" and of that law and the prophets which He adopted and confirmed when He said, "Till heaven and earth pass, one jot or one tittle shall in no wise pass from the law, till all be fulfilled," *Matthew* 5:18.

If "Redemption" meant only the return of Israel from Captivity, **there was no need for Christ to die:** indeed no need for Him to leave Heaven at all to accomplish it! Israel could have been brought back as easily and as readily as Judah was brought back from Babylon.

But "redemption" has a much bigger meaning than that! Sacrifice, atonement, and the shedding of blood were necessary.

"And without shedding of blood is no remission" *Hebrews* 9:22. And the writer to the Hebrews is quite definite as to how Redemption comes.

"Neither by the blood of goats and calves, *but by his own blood he entered in once into the holy place, having obtained eternal redemption for us*" 9:12.

What marvellous words are here! How clear and also how positive they are!

Dare I remind you that the writer is writing to the Hebrews, and he says, *"Having obtained eternal redemption for us"* Hebrews 9:12.

O, the magnificence and glory of this tremendous statement. Do we take in all it says and means?

Is there a man amongst us who dares to give these words their full and obvious import?

Is there a meaning in them higher than that commonly supposed?

I am quite aware that there may be a hill beyond what we can see, *but have we taken into account the hill we can see, the one straight before our eyes?*

Sometimes on searching in a room for something we fail to find it, and a relative says, "I have just seen it, I know it is there," but because of our preoccupation we fail to see it!

Are we like that when we come to God's book? Are we reading into this passage something that is not there, and closing our eyes to something that is there?

Remember the High Priest's words, "Die for the people, and that the whole nation perish not . . . being high priest that year, *he prophesied that Jesus should die for that nation"* John 11:50-51.

And Christ our Lord was equally clear. Just before He offered Himself up, He told the disciples the secret of it all: "This is my body which is given *for you* . . . This cup is the new testament in my blood, which is shed *for you"* Luke 22:19-20.

The offering, the shedding of the blood was necessary for the remission, *and the final cry, "It is finished," proclaimed the accomplishment of Israel's redemption.*

God's way of equality is not the breaking down of the Israel mark, and the Israel quality to the level of other nations. O, no, He has an infinitely better way! *His way is the bringing up of the other nations to and into Israel!*

Man's way is to *level down*, and scores of preachers preach it, *but God's way is to level up!*

And He is using Israel for that purpose, till bye and bye there will be left only that Israel, and He is their King!

But all may come in and join Israel. And that is how He will finally fix things up, if they will. Please observe that word "*May.*" I do not say they will.

The bringing in of God's Kingdom is not to be by a general levelling down, but by a gradual lifting up, begun in one man, Abraham and his race, continued with never-ceasing purpose through all the vicissitudes of that race, God working in them to make them His Holy people, priests of the Lord, *and then through them and their exalted priestly ministry to lift up the Nations, admitting them to the Israel favours and the Israel blessings as they accept the Gospel message and take Israel's God for theirs.*

Is there any man that has got anything to say against that? *The fact is God is going to form for Himself a Kingdom upon earth, and He begins it in Israel, then in the other Nations through Israel.*

One of our opponents recently said, in trying to depreciate our arguments and conclusions: "That refers to the Millennium."

Most assuredly if it is not the Millennium, it will make it so, for that will bring it in.

But why should that be considered an argument which puts us out of court? Is not the Millennium a real thing? A genuine happening, and upon this earth? *The Millennium is not in the skies!*

It is here, and comes to people living upon this earth, with real tangible bodies like our own, who have children in constant succession, cultivate their gardens, sow their fields, reap their corn, harvest their fruits, and make the desolate earth to become as the garden of Eden.

There are beasts too, though *God has stopped their mouths.* There are lion and the bear, but they are ravenous no more. They eat straw like the ox, the little child shall play on the hole of the asp, and the weaned child shall put his hand on the cockatrice's den. "They shall not hurt nor destroy in all My holy mountain: for the earth" (not heaven, please) "shall be full of the knowledge of the LORD, as the waters cover the sea" *Isaiah* 11:6-9.

Every bit of that is literal. *It is all real!*

Redemption! What is it? May I suggest that it is more than individual salvation in as much as the nation is greater than the individual.

Salvation is to and for the individual. Redemption is to and for the nation.

Redemption in its first phrase was seen at Calvary. *In its last phase it is, to those then living, Salvation to every individual in the nation!* (To the Gentiles as well as Israel, Salvation is offered to the individual, and all who accept are joined to Israel and become part and parcel of Israel wherever they may be.)

Take the single saved individual, multiply him by ten thousand, by ten million, estimate the nation more exactly and minutely than in any census ever taken, leaving out not a single one: *there you have redemption in its fullest meaning, and come to full accomplishment.*

Do you wonder that God Himself goes into raptures of joy at its contemplation?

And man would if he knew it and believed it. But it is coming in the future if the Word of God is true.

Listen to these tremendous words of God: "*In those days, and in that time, saith the LORD, the iniquity of Israel shall be sought for, and there shall be none; and the sins of Judah, and they shall not be found*" *Jeremiah* 50:20.

An absolutely staggering statement. Most assuredly this is something beyond the commonly received interpretation, and it comes to both houses, most clearly showing that God is speaking of the literal houses of Israel and Judah.

Now Christ's mission was to bring in that righteousness.

The angel that spoke to Daniel referring to the purpose of our Lord's coming said it was "*To finish the transgression, and to make an end of sins*" (will you note that, please?) "*And to make reconciliation for iniquity,*" that part we have understood, but I greatly question whether we have understood the closing words: **"and to bring in everlasting righteousness."**

Now it would be of no use to announce that Christ was going to bring in everlasting righteousness in Heaven! *It is upon earth*!

These were not Daniel's words. They were the words of the heavenly visitant who came to give him skill and understanding.

Isaiah 60:21 says, "*Thy people also shall be all righteous: they shall inherit the land for ever*" (Ferrar Fenton says, "shall conquer the earth"), "*the branch of my planting, the work of my hands*, **that I may be glorified.**" Notice it is "Thy people."

This cannot mean heaven, that cannot be conquered! And its inhabitants are already righteous. It is an announcement of the redeeming of God's ancient people. **All made righteous**!

If this is so we may now understand those very forceful words in *Isaiah* 45:17, *"But Israel shall be saved in the LORD with an everlasting salvation: ye shall not be ashamed nor confounded world without end."*

Now the word "Redeemed" means all that. And the last verse of the chapter nearly takes our breath away by the tremendous nature of its claim.

"In the LORD shall all the seed of Israel be justified and shall glory."

That is not my statement! *It is the word of the Living God!*

"All the seed of Israel." Think of it. There we have redemption in full operation. The writer to the Hebrews (mark who it is to, *the Hebrews*), referring to our Lord's sacrifice of Himself, says in chapter 9:12, "Neither by the blood of goats and calves, but by his own blood he entered in once into the holy place, *having obtained eternal redemption for us."* Marvellous words indeed. Is it possible that their full meaning has escaped us?

The promise came to Zion 2,000 years ago, "Thus saith the LORD, Ye have sold yourselves for nought; *and ye shall be redeemed without money" Isaiah* 52:3.

And *Isaiah* 62:12, speaking of the same people, says: *"And they shall call them, The holy people, The redeemed of the LORD."*

And chapter 51:11 says: "Therefore the redeemed of the LORD shall return, and come with singing unto Zion; . . . they shall obtain gladness and joy; and sorrow and mourning shall flee away."

Isaiah 60:16 says that Israel shall know that He is both their Saviour and their Redeemer.

"And thou shalt know that I the LORD am thy Saviour and thy Redeemer, the mighty One of Jacob." This is a promise of the future not yet fully realised.

And chapter 49:25-26 says that the whole of the world shall know of it. "I will contend with him that contendeth with thee, and I will save thy children. And I will feed them that oppress thee with their own flesh; . . . *and all flesh shall know that I the LORD am thy Saviour and thy Redeemer, the mighty One of Jacob."*

Saviour individually, Redeemer of the nation, and all flesh to know it!

As to the time of trial which we have to go through beforehand, and in preparation for it, the Scriptures are not silent, but the end is assured.

If our evangelists could really see what all this means *and believed it*, it would be the greatest eye-opener they have ever had.

These are not promises to a few individuals of strong and exceptional faith as they teach, **they are promises to a whole nation, a whole wicked nation, men, women and children!**

Say you: "It will take hundreds of years to accomplish this!" Indeed, it would if man had to do the work. But he has not! *God does it, and does it in His own way*!

Someone says, "How?" Even that is not a secret altogether hidden from us in the Word. *It may be known!*

So then, Christ the Redeemer has indeed come to redeem Israel, exactly as the two disciples thought, though they were in error as to the manner of the redeeming: *and most decidedly He has done the work He came to do*: and with that also He was "The Lamb of God which taketh away the sin of the world."

While seeing and acknowledging the latter, let us rejoice with unbounded joy in the former, for God Himself does so, and calls upon all creation to join Him.

"O Israel, thou shalt not be forgotten of me . . . return unto me; *for I have redeemed thee. Sing, O ye heavens, for the LORD hath done it: shout, ye lower parts of the earth: break forth into singing, ye mountains, O forest, and every tree therein:*" (and here is the cause of the rejoicing), "*for the LORD hath redeemed Jacob, and glorified Himself in Israel*" Isaiah 44:21-23.

Most assuredly this has not yet been completely fulfilled. But as truly as God is faithful it will be, even down to the last jot and tittle. And it is quite possible that it is so near that there are thousands in Israel now alive who will live to see it, go through it, and glory in it.